Punctuation and Spelling

Rebecca Vickers

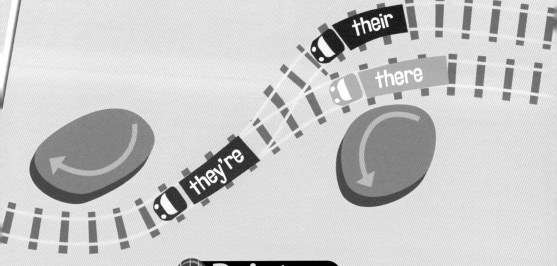

Raintree is an imprint of Capstone Global Library Limited, a company incorporated in England and Wales having its registered office at 7 Pilgrim Street, London, EC4V 6LB – Registered company number: 6695582

To contact Raintree, please phone 0845 6044371, fax + 44 (0) 1865 312263, or email myorders@raintreepublishers.co.uk.

Edited by Andrew Farrow, Laura Hensley, Vaarunika Dharmapala, Helen Cox Cannons
Designed by Philippa Jenkins
Original illustrations © Capstone Global Library Ltd
Illustrated by Capstone Global Library Ltd
Picture research by Tracy Cummins
Production by Sophia Argyris
Printed in China by Leo Paper Products Ltd

ISBN 978 1 406 26162 2
17 16 15 14 13
10 9 8 7 6 5 4 3 2 1

British Library Cataloguing in Publication Data
Vickers, Rebecca.
    Punctuation and spelling. -- (Find your way with words)
    1. English language--Punctuation--Juvenile literature. 2. English language--Orthography and spelling--Juvenile literature.
    I. Title II. Series
    421.1-dc23

Acknowledgements
We would like to thank the following for permission to reproduce photographs:
Alamy p. 29 top (© Jamie Carstairs); AP Photo p. 13 (Dave Caulkin); Capstone Library p. 16; Getty Images pp. 34 left (Nordic Photos), 45 (JEWEL SAMAD/AFP); Library of Congress Prints and Photographs Division p. 23; newscom pp. 19 (KRT PHOTOGRAPH VIA LOUISA MAY ALCOTT MEMORIAL ASSOCIATION), 29 bottom (Clem Murray/Philadelphia Inquirer/MCT); Shutterstock pp. 5 (© AVAVA), 6 (© Aaron Amat), 9 (© Aaron Amat), 11 (© Simone van den Berg), 15 middle (© AlikeYou), 15 bottom (© Glenda M. Powers), 15 top (© kostudio), 17 (© pjhpix), 18 (© dedMazay), 21 (© James Clarke), 24 (© Aaron Amat), 25 (© Dragon Images), 27 (© auremar), 31 (© mkabakov), 33 (© Margot Petrowski), 34 right (© Marcel Mooij), 35 (© Lukich), 36 caribou (© Sylvie Bouchard), 36 sleigh (© 3dfoto), 36 wool (© MARGRIT HIRSCH), 38 (© Fotokostic), 39 (© Yuri Arcurs), 41 (© blewisphotography), 43 deer (© Vishnevskiy Vasily), 43 goose (© E.O), 43 mouse (© Eric Isselée), sheep (© Eric Isselée), 47 (© Gert Johannes Jacobus Very), 49 (© Madlen), 49 (© Hong Vo), 49 (© MilousSK), 50 (© Andrew Ward), 51 (© David Majestic); Superstock p. 30 (© Melvin Longhurst).

Back cover image of the letters in the words 'fame' and 'famous' reproduced by Capstone Global Library.

We would like to thank Joanna John for her invaluable help in the preparation of this book.

Every effort has been made to contact copyright holders of material reproduced in this book. Any omissions will be rectified in subsequent printings if notice is given to the publisher.

Contents

Getting it right

Language is about communication. How we write and what we say are both part of this process. Two of the most important aspects of language use and communication are proper punctuation and accurate spelling. Whether your written work is a school essay, a note to a friend, a job application, or instructions for a science experiment, accuracy and attention to detail in your writing will help make your meaning clear.

Why are spelling and punctuation important?

It's not just a matter of making yourself understandable; you need to understand others as well. Reading information that is badly spelled or incorrectly punctuated can be annoying, confusing, or, in the case of technical writing, even dangerous. Here are some other reasons why getting writing right is important:

- Correct use of standard spelling and punctuation makes written material easier to read. This is true, both in the sense of easily recognizing the words being used and understanding which words relate to each other.
- Poor spelling and punctuation give the reader a bad impression of the writer. It can bring into question how much the writer cares about the material being written. This can really work against you when it comes to school work, CVs, and job applications.
- When you make the effort to write something, even if it is just a casual email to a friend, you want the reader to concentrate on the content. If you use poor punctuation, then your reader will pay more attention to your lack of skills rather than the content of the message.
- When you are writing something factual and informative, your reader might also wonder if your information is correct if your spelling and punctuation are not accurate.

QUICK TIP

Glossary

This book has a Glossary on pages 53-54. If you see a word you don't understand, check the Glossary to see if the word is there. If it isn't, try a good dictionary (see page 7).

Getting a point across

An author's descriptive language can only be successful, as it is here, if the reader understands it. Using standard English punctuation and spelling will make this easier:

> At the hitch-bars along the street a few heavy work-horses, harnessed to farm wagons, shivered under their blankets. About the station everything was quiet, for there would not be another train in until night.

From *O Pioneers!* by Willa Cather (1873–1947), published by Houghton Mifflin Company, 1913.

Even when the simplest instructions are written with bad grammar, spelling, and punctuation, you can find them hard to follow.

Learning about punctuation and spelling

The best way to learn how to use correct punctuation marks is to use them in the structure of written sentences. This structure is called "syntax". In the first part of this book, we will describe the three types of punctuation marks, with an explanation of the rules for their use:

- Punctuation at the end of a sentence – These punctuation marks are used to finish a sentence and separate it from the next one. They include the full stop, question mark, and exclamation mark.
- Punctuation inside a sentence – These punctuation marks are used to divide parts of a sentence. They include the comma, semicolon, colon, dash, round and square brackets, ellipsis, and quotation marks (also called inverted commas, or speech marks).
- Punctuating words – These punctuation marks affect individual words. They include the apostrophe, hyphen, boldface, and italic.

The second part of this book will focus on how to get to grips with spelling. It includes some of the most important spelling rules, advice about plurals, tips about spelling and pronunciation, and fun memory tricks to learn.

QUICK TIP

Look it up!

A dictionary is the best place to find a correct spelling. Once you find the word you want, don't just check the spelling. Check what part of speech it is, and look at the definition to make sure it is really the word you want. If you are so unsure that even finding the word in a dictionary seems impossible, try using an online search engine. Put in your best idea of the spelling, and see if the results include likely examples. You can then check those words in an online dictionary.

Using a dictionary

Dictionaries are reference books that list thousands of words and their meanings in alphabetical order. Good dictionaries can be found as books, websites, and as smartphone apps. There are also specialist dictionaries for individual subjects, such as medicine and art.

Each full word entry gives the correct spelling of the word, any different spellings, the pronunciation, and the meanings or usages of the word. It might also include principal verb parts, plurals, and related words in the same word family. Sometimes, information about the history of the word is provided. All of the abbreviations and pronunciation symbols used, and an explanation of how the entries are set out, are always given at the beginning of the dictionary.

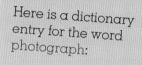

Here is a dictionary entry for the word *photograph*:

pronunciation and any alternate pronunciation divided into syllables with accent marks

parts of speech for the entry word

entry word

verb endings

transitive verb form word meaning

sentence showing usage of meaning

photograph (fō´tə gräf´, -graf´) *n.,v.,* **-graphed, -graphing.** *n.***1.** image taken by one of several photographic processes. *vt.* **2.** to take photograph of . *vi.* **3.** to practise photography. 4. to be photographed or be the subject of a photograph. *The flowers photographed beautifully.* **photographer** *n.* **–photographic** *a.* **–photography** *n.* [*Gk* photo- +-graph 1839]

noun form word meaning

intransitive verb form word meanings

history of word, with language of origin of the parts and date of first use

other words in the same word family that also have entries in the dictionary

When you speak to other people, you punctuate your speech in many ways. You may pause or change your facial expressions, your tone of voice, or the rhythm of your sentences. This helps listeners to understand you; they can even ask you questions or get you to repeat something. When you are reading, these verbal and visual clues are not available. The punctuation marks used in written English act in the same way as expressions do for speech.

Written work is divided by punctuation marks into sentences. A sentence needs to make sense as the expression of an idea. Each complete sentence must have at least a subject (a noun and words related to it) and a predicate (a verb and words related to it). This is called a main clause. The first word in a sentence always starts with a capital letter and ends with one of the three punctuation marks described in this chapter.

The full stop

A full stop (.) is the punctuation mark that is most often used to signal the end of a complete sentence. Like all final punctuation, the function of a full stop is to separate one sentence from the next. This avoids run-on sentences, where two ideas expressed in main clauses are mistakenly combined with only a comma or no punctuation separating them:

WRONG: Layla wants to learn to play the drums, Holly hopes to start guitar lessons.

As these two ideas are both main clauses, they cannot be separated by a comma. They need to stand on their own as two sentences, or be connected using a linking word, such as the conjunctions and or but. They could also be separated by a semicolon (see page 18).

RIGHT: Layla wants to learn to play the drums. Holly hopes to start guitar lessons.

RIGHT: Layla wants to learn to play the drums and Holly hopes to start guitar lessons.

RIGHT: Layla wants to learn to play the drums, but Holly hopes to start guitar lessons.

Full stops should never be used to punctuate an incomplete sentence, known as a fragment:

WRONG: Holly hopes to start guitar lessons [complete sentence]. Or learn another stringed instrument [fragment].

Auditions for the school play Friday at 4p.m. by Mr Phillips will be in the drama studio next to the dining hall.

Is the play called *Friday at 4p.m.*? Did Mr Phillips write it, or is he choosing the actors for the parts? What time are the auditions? Bad punctuation makes this notice really hard to work

Stream of conciousness

Some authors developed a style of writing called "stream of consciousness" to reproduce the random and confusing nature of human thought. Punctuation may be used, but sentences often run-on together or are only fragments or individual words. It was thought that not following the usual structure would be a good way to imitate the way people think. This quote is from a novel narrated by a 16-year-old boy, Holden Caulfield:

What I mean is, lots of time you don't know what interests you most till you start talking about something that doesn't interest you most.

From *The Catcher in the Rye* by J.D. Salinger (1919–2010), published by Little, Brown and Company, 1951.

The question mark

A question mark (?) is the punctuation mark used at the end of a sentence that asks a question. This is called an "interrogative sentence". There are three main types:

1. A sentence where the answer is yes or no – A sentence of this type inverts the normal word order to ask a question. If the normal word order of a sentence is Kamal is eating curry and rice tonight, then a question of this type would be Is Kamal eating curry and rice tonight?

2. A sentence that asks a who, what, which, where, why, when, or how question – These are questions that prompt a fuller answer. For example, if the question is What is Kamal eating tonight?, then the answer cannot be a simple yes or no. These sentences also invert the normal word order.

3. If you are writing something where you directly report the speech of someone who has asked a question, then this also ends in a question mark: Anna asked me, "Do you like chocolate sauce on your ice cream?" However, if you are reporting what the person said, then you do not need a question mark: Anna asked me if I liked chocolate sauce on my ice cream.

The exclamation mark

The exclamation mark (!) is a punctuation mark used at the end of a sentence that expresses surprise, excitement, or strong feeling. It can also be used after interjections, such as Wow!, Help!, or Ouch! A sentence that ends in an exclamation mark is referred to as an "exclamation". Sometimes exclamations begin with words like how or what: for example, What an idiot Archie is!

EAT YOUR WORDS

No need to exclaim!

In most school essays and reports, using exclamation marks is too informal in style, like using slang or other informal language.

Wrong: I really like Shakespeare's plays!

Right: Shakespeare is recognized as one of the best dramatists to have ever lived.

QUICK TIP

No space needed

Full stops, question marks, and exclamation marks should always be placed directly after the last letters of the last words of the sentences they punctuate. Never leave a space before the final punctuation.

In informal writing, such as texts, tweets, social network posts, and emails to friends, using informal spelling and multiple punctuation marks for effect is fine. However, this kind of usage is never acceptable in more formal writing, such as school work.

What r u wearing 2nite??

OMG!! No clue!!

Punctuation inside a sentence is used to divide or interrupt the flow of thought. Not every sentence needs internal punctuation. It should only be used to increase the clarity of what is written.

The comma

A comma (,) is a punctuation mark used in sentences to separate words from each other. There are several ways to use commas:

- Series or list commas – These are used to separate three or more individual words, or groups of words, in a type of list: Stacy bought apples, bananas, and pears. Angelo takes the bus to school, the underground to the gym, and the train to visit his grandma. The groups of words can even be complete sentences, but there must be at least three with the last element connected with a conjunction, such as and or or: Alice wore a white tutu, Cleo wore a pink tutu, and Helen wore a black tutu. Series or list commas are also used to separate descriptive words that modify a noun: The gorilla's large, sad, bloodshot eyes stared at me. The use of the comma before the connecting word in a series list is sometimes omitted. Note that no comma is used between the last adjective and the noun.

- Commas with conjunctions to join two sentences – This type of comma can only be used with a joining or linking word, such as the conjunctions and, but, or, while, and yet. Here is an example: Jonas likes cycling, but he would rather go skateboarding. Both parts are complete, and could stand on their own as sentences. Remember, you can never have a comma between two sentences unless there is a linking conjunction.

- Bracketing or parenthetical commas – These commas usually work in pairs to separate off a piece of information. This information is additional to the main idea of the sentence, and can be taken out to leave a complete sentence. In these examples, the words inside the bracketing commas add extra information that interrupts the flow of the sentence: His Great Aunt Marjorie, who lived in London, worked as a government spy during the 1950s. Sometimes the extra words appear at the beginning or the end of the sentence. In those cases, only one comma needs to be used. For example, at the beginning: After the delay, all of the passengers for the Miami flight moved to a different gate, or at the end: The volcano is located in the centre of the island, thirty kilometres inland.

Can you read around?

One way to test if a pair of bracketing commas is used correctly is to "read around" the text inside the commas. In other words, does the sentence still make sense without the bracketed words? Here is an example: **John**, who was only 15, **was the youngest competitor**. The bold words make sense without the information in the bracketing commas.

Can you imagine a bestseller about punctuation? British writer Lynne Truss is the author of just such a book. Her *Eats, Shoots & Leaves: The Zero Tolerance Approach to Punctuation* has sold over three million copies worldwide.

- Commas that separate a direct address of someone – This type of comma is used to set off someone's name or title to show direct speech: Prime Minister, I am honoured to meet you.
- Commas that replace words – This less common use of the comma is different from the other three, as it replaces words previously used in the sentence. This means that the same words don't need to be repeated. Here are two examples: Some of the group wanted to go to the local theme park for the class day out; others, to the local zoo. In this example, the comma after others replaces the words wanted to go. In the next sentence, commas are used twice to replace the words likes listening to, which would have to be inserted after Miles and Charlie: Emma likes listening to hip-hop and alt country, Miles, world music and folk, and Charlie, heavy metal and rock.

EAT YOUR WORDS

Commas "never" and "always" rules

- ALWAYS use a comma after the words yes or no when used at the beginning of a sentence in reply to a question unless the yes or no is followed by a verb: Yes, I want to go to the pool tomorrow, but No is my answer to your request.

- NEVER put a comma in front of the word that to bracket off bits of a sentence.

- ALWAYS use a comma in front of a group of words that starts with which.

- ALWAYS use a comma to bracket off information after a proper noun: They were lucky to see the swimmer Michael Phelps, who has won many gold medals.

- NEVER use a series or listing comma unless the commas could be replaced with the words and or or.

- ALWAYS use a conjunction, such as but or and, when a comma is used to join parts of a sentence.

Commas in numbers

In numbers with more than three numerals (numbers over 999), a comma is inserted after every three numerals counting from right to left, for example: 1,300 and 25,700,425. There are two exceptions to this:

1. Date years of four numerals never have a comma: 1776 or 1939.
2. In most scientific and mathematical writing, no commas are used in numbers. However, some scientific writing leaves a narrow space in the place where a comma would be inserted.

Let's eat, Grandpa!

Let's eat Grandpa!

Putting in a comma can really change the meaning of a sentence! It would be even better to put the addressing word, Grandpa, at the beginning of the sentence. Addressing words like this are always followed by a comma: Grandpa, let's eat!

The colon

A colon (:) is a punctuation mark used in a sentence to show that the information in the words following it help explain or add to the information that comes before. In most cases, there is a complete sentence before the colon, while the words after the colon can be another sentence, a list, or even one word: Zach really loves fruit: apples, oranges, bananas, and particularly grapes. As is demonstrated in this example, the information before the colon is usually general, and the information after the colon gives more details, examples, or explanation.

Here is an example of one word coming after a colon: There is one thing that all professional footballers fear: injury.

EAT YOUR WORDS

Colon "always" and "never" rules

- ALWAYS put the colon immediately after a word with no space, and leave a space after it before the next word.
- NEVER follow a colon directly with any other punctuation mark.
- NEVER use a colon at the end of a chapter title or chapter subhead in written work.
- ALWAYS use a colon when writing down a book title to separate the title from its subtitle, even if there is no colon on the cover or title page: The Chrysanthemum Throne: A History of the Emperors of Japan.

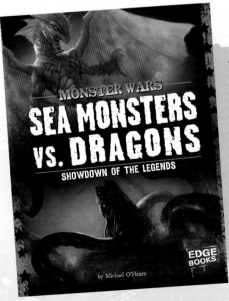

MONSTER WARS

SEA MONSTERS VS. DRAGONS

SHOWDOWN OF THE LEGENDS

by Michael O'Hearn

EDGE BOOKS

Even though the cover of this book does not show a colon between the title and the subtitle, when you write the title, you always show this punctuation between the two parts: Sea Monsters vs. Dragons: Showdown of the Legends.

Special colon uses

There are a few special uses for colons. Colons are used without spaces in mathematical ratios: 3:1. This would be written out as three to one. Colons are also sometimes used in writing endnote, footnote, and bibliography entries for books.

Colons are often used to divide information from the general to the specific: Nathan loves going to watch any live music: rock, folk, jazz, or classical. In this sentence, the term "live music" is the general, and the names of all the types of live music after the colon are the specific examples.

The semicolon

A semicolon (;) is a punctuation mark mainly used between two groups of words that could stand as independent sentences. For the usage to be correct, the text in the two sentences must be so closely related that it is better for them to be together. Here is an example: Josie wears her grandma's watch; it helps keep the memories alive.

EAT YOUR WORDS

Semicolon "always" and "never" rules

- NEVER use a semicolon if there is a connecting word like and or but.

- NEVER use a semicolon unless two complete and closely related sentences are being separated.

- ALWAYS think before using a semicolon. It is often not the most appropriate or accurate choice.

QUICK TIP

Semicolons instead of commas

It is possible to decide to use a semicolon when there are so many commas in a sentence that it becomes confusing. In that case, to make it clearer, the main break or breaks can have the commas replaced by semicolons. Here is an example: The actor wore a tall, black hat; a red jacket, which someone had put on him in the second act; and black, knee-high boots.

Be careful when using a chainsaw; all your fingers should be well clear.

It's not his fingers I'm worried about; it's my legs!

Semicolons in use

Works of literature, such as Louisa May Alcott's novel *Little Women*, often make good use of semicolons in complex sentences with many commas. In the second sentence below, there are two semicolons: one dividing two complete sentences, and one to clarify a group of words with many commas.

> Very few letters were written in those hard times that were not touching, especially those which fathers sent home. In this one little was said of the hardships endured, the dangers faced, or the homesickness conquered; it was a cheerful, hopeful letter, full of lively descriptions of camp life, marches, and military news; and only at the end did the writer's heart overflow with fatherly love and longing for the little girls at home.

From *Little Women* by Louisa May Alcott (1832–1888), first published in 1868.

The American Civil War had only been over for four years when *Little Women* was published. Louisa May Alcott (shown here) was familiar with the heartbreak many families suffered while their loved ones were away fighting, many never to return.

The dash

A dash (–) is a punctuation mark used to separate off a part of a sentence that strongly interrupts the rest of the flow. In this way, dashes used in pairs are like bracketing commas, but the words they set off need to represent a more powerful break. However, like bracketing commas, it must be possible to "read around" the text inside the dashes. The rest of the words must form a complete sentence: When the two teams met, they both seemed sure of victory – there was no doubting it – because each of them was a group champion.

Sometimes the interruption doesn't come in the middle of the sentence, but at the end. When this is the case, only one dash is needed: Woody swore that the cake was already gone when he got home – at least that's what he said. This use of a strong interruption of the text at the end of a sentence is a quite informal style, and is probably only appropriate in creative writing or dialogue.

QUICK TIP

Number ranges

In certain circumstances, the appropriate punctuation to use when representing a range of numbers or dates is a dash, not a hyphen. For example, Queen Victoria lived 1819-1901 is correct. In this case, the dash represents the words from and to. So, it could also be written Queen Victoria lived from 1819 to 1901. It is wrong to mix the two styles so, if the word from is used, then there cannot be a dash between the two dates. **Wrong**: Queen Victoria lived from 1819-1901.

EAT YOUR WORDS

Dash "always" and "never" rules

- NEVER leave a dash at the end of a line of text.

- NEVER use a dash in place of a hyphen (see page 28) or directly after any other punctuation mark.

- ALWAYS think carefully before using dashes. They are often not the most accurate or appropriate choice of punctuation mark to use.

A dash can also be used to replace the words between and and. For example, Her guess is that there are 430–560 jelly beans in the jar. It would also be correct to say Her guess is that there are between 430 and 560 jelly beans

There are 283 exactly!

No, there are between 550 and 580!

Round brackets

Round brackets (( )), which are also called parentheses, are punctuation marks that are always used in pairs. Like bracketing commas and dashes, they are used to separate bits of information from the rest of a complete sentence. Round brackets can be used to set off both strong and weak interruptions to the flow of a sentence: Fergus lived on a farm (with both sheep and cattle) located just north of the Scottish border. They can also be used to set off information that adds to a sentence, but cannot easily be written into it, such as dates: Winston Churchill (1874–1965) was Prime Minister during most of World War II (1939–45).

Square brackets

Square brackets ([ ]) are punctuation marks that are always used in pairs. Their main function is to separate off information which is being added to a direct quotation. The material in the square brackets is not part of the quotation. Here is an example from a quote by economist John Maynard Keynes: But, like Odysseus, the President [Woodrow Wilson] looked wiser when he was seated.

Quotation marks

Quotation marks (" "), also known as speech marks or inverted commas, are the punctuation marks used in pairs to show directly quoted material, to set off dialogue, and to emphasize certain words in text. When quotation marks are used, it shows that the words inside them are direct quotes from a person or publication. Directly reported conversation, or dialogue, is also set off using quotation marks.

EAT YOUR WORDS

Single or double?

There are both single and double quotation marks. Different countries, education systems, and book publishers have their favourite style of use. This series of books favours double quotes. If you need to mark off a quote within a quote, or a group of words within dialogue, use the most popular style for the first quote marks and then the less popular style inside: "I love mountain climbing," said Evie. "It always makes me think, 'Wow, I'm lucky to be alive,' every time I get to the top." Find more information on how to punctuate dialogue and conversation in another book in this series, *Making Better Sentences*.

Sic means "not my mistake"!

Another special use of square brackets is with the Latin word sic, which means "thus". This word in square brackets is used to point out that a spelling, factual, or grammatical error in a text that is being quoted was really in the original quote. In other words, the mistake belongs to someone else: The sign near the driveway said No Parkin [**sic**].

Daisy Ashford (1881–1972) was only nine in 1890 when she wrote her short novel *The Young Visiters*. It was published in 1919, with her original misspelling of "visiters" kept. When people write about this book, they use sic to show that the misspelling is actually in the book title and is not their mistake: One of her favourite books is *The Young Visiters* [**sic**] by Daisy Ashford.

Giving emphasis

Sometimes it is useful to emphasize a word or phrase that you want to explain further, and quotation marks can be used to do that. That kind of emphasis can also be used to show humour or displeasure: It can be said that "handsome" is not a word you would use to describe his face. Quotation marks are also used in footnotes, endnotes, and bibliography entries to set off the titles of journal articles and chapters in books.

The ellipsis

An ellipsis (...) is a punctuation mark used to show that something has been omitted from a direct quote. The three full stops in a row are also called omission marks.

If you use an ellipsis, it is important that you do not change the meaning of the original writing by the omissions you make. For example, here is a statement from a critic's review of a film: Even if I live to be 100, it is unlikely I will ever see a film with more truly unbelievable military characters in a wrongheaded wartime storyline. Here is the same sentence with ellipses replacing some text: Even if I live to be 100, it is unlikely I will ever see a film with more truly ... military characters in a ... wartime storyline. If this new quote was used to advertise the film, would it represent the reviewer's true opinions?

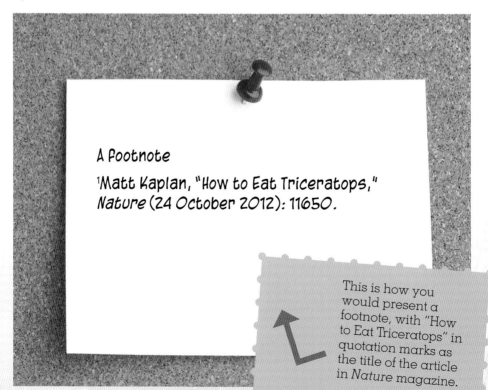

A Footnote

¹Matt Kaplan, "How to Eat Triceratops," *Nature* (24 October 2012): 11650.

This is how you would present a footnote, with "How to Eat Triceratops" in quotation marks as the title of the article in *Nature* magazine.

When you are writing informally in texts or emails, using ellipses can give your message a conversational feel or represent unfinished thoughts. However, in formal writing, there are only a few correct or appropriate uses.

I know what you mean ... I sometimes feel it's just too much trouble to stay friends with everyone ... But I don't mean you, of course!

Word punctuation

Some punctuation marks are used to change or modify individual words. These include the apostrophe, the hyphen, the full stop used with abbreviations, and changes to the way words look, such as capitals, boldface, and italic.

The apostrophe

The apostrophe (') is a punctuation mark with three completely different uses.

Contractions

The first use is to make contractions, which are shortened forms of words with some of the letters left out and replaced by an apostrophe. Most contractions are formed from two words. Here are some examples:

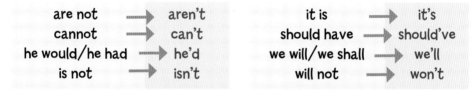

are not	→	aren't		it is	→	it's
cannot	→	can't		should have	→	should've
he would/he had	→	he'd		we will/we shall	→	we'll
is not	→	isn't		will not	→	won't

The apostrophe is almost always placed where the dropped letters were removed. It signals to the reader that the word is a contraction rather than a word that looks the same, such as we'll and well and he'll and hell.

Possession

The second use for the apostrophe is with the letter s to show possession. Possessives are noun forms that show when something belongs to someone or something. This noun form is usually created by adding an apostrophe and an s. Here are a few examples: Anisa's sisters all have red hair; The children's book section had small chairs and tables; Max's mountain bike was stolen. There are three exceptions to this rule:

- If the noun concerned is already plural and ends in s, then another s is not added, only an apostrophe: Sam lost two weeks' work when his computer crashed.
- A proper name that ends in s doesn't need another s to show possession if that isn't the way you would pronounce it. You only need to add an apostrophe to make the possessive form: Socrates' football career ended in 1989.
- Pronouns never show the possessive form by adding an apostrophe and an s, for example: We need to find our keys, He went with his brother, or The alligator opened its mouth.

Don't get "it" wrong!

Probably the most confusing use of the apostrophe is with the word it. The word it made into a possessive would look just the same as the contraction of it is or it has into it's. So, in this case, as it is with the other pronouns, the possessive form never has an apostrophe.

RIGHT: The committee always carries out its decisions.

WRONG: The skateboard wasn't in it's normal place.

RIGHT: It's [It is] the place where I usually put the skateboard.

Society
for the
preservation
of the
APOSTROPHE

Many people find the misuse of the apostrophe very irritating. Some groups want to get rid of possessive apostrophes entirely as they are so often used incorrectly.

Shortened words

The third use of the apostrophe is to replace the missing letters in shortened words. There are certain words where the long form of the word is now commonly shortened. In the past, words like phone, as the shortened form of telephone, and flu, as the shortened form of influenza, were written with apostrophes where the dropped bit used to be (for example, 'phone). Apostrophes are now rarely used in this way. It is considered old-fashioned and unnecessary, unless the shortened word is still not considered an acceptable word on its own such as the informal usage 'bout to mean about.

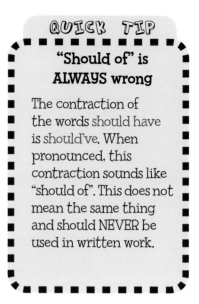

QUICK TIP

"Should of" is ALWAYS wrong

The contraction of the words should have is should've. When pronounced, this contraction sounds like "should of". This does not mean the same thing and should NEVER be used in written work.

The hyphen

A hyphen (-) is a punctuation mark with four main uses:

- A hyphen can be used at the end of a line after part of a word to show that the word has been split between two lines. This is awkward, and should be avoided if at all possible.
- Hyphens are often used to make words like the adjective African-American. These are called compound words. The rules here are very changeable, so check a dictionary. Sometimes a dictionary will give a choice of hyphenation, one word, or two separate words. If that is the case then it is your personal preference which to use: web-site, website, web site.
- When two adjectives are used to describe a noun, sometimes it is clearer to hyphenate the two words to show they are being used together. Here are two examples: The film had a very slow-moving plot; The blue-green glass bowl looked great on the shelf.
- Hyphens are sometimes used with word additions, like anti-, re-, pre-, and non- when they are added to the beginning of a word. These additions are called prefixes. When the next word starts with a capital letter, then a hyphen is always used: anti-Western, non-Catholic, pro-Roman. Usually, if the prefix ends in a vowel and the next word starts with a vowel, you need a hyphen: re-open, pre-empt. If the prefix ends in the same consonant as the word, a hyphen is sometimes used: non-negotiable. Again, there are no firm rules here, so you may need to check your choices in a dictionary.

RUG'S + CARPETS

RUG SALE

Shops, small businesses, and even large organizations can often use possessive apostrophes wrongly on their publicity signs.

Four Seasons Cleaner's

Mon - Fri	7:30 - 6:00
Sat	9:00 4:0
Sun.	CLOSED

Italics

With so much written work being done on computers, individual words can be changed by the use of different typefaces. The italic typeface, *like this*, is used for several purposes:

- Italics are used to replace underlining in footnotes, endnotes, and bibliography references.
- Italics are also used for the titles of books, magazines, films, and musical pieces.
- Italics can be used to give a word or phrase emphasis. Here is an example: Your appointment was *last* Tuesday, not today.
- Foreign words not normally used in English should be shown in italics, for example, *mal de mer* (French for seasickness).
- Genus and species names in biology are most often shown in italics, for example, *Homo sapiens* (modern man).

QUICK TIP

Exception to the rule

The religious holy book names the Bible, the Torah, and the Qur'an are never shown in italic.

The names of boats, ships, aircraft, and spacecraft are always, when possible, shown in italic in written work, for example, The *Titanic*, The *Mary Rose*, HMS *Invincible*.

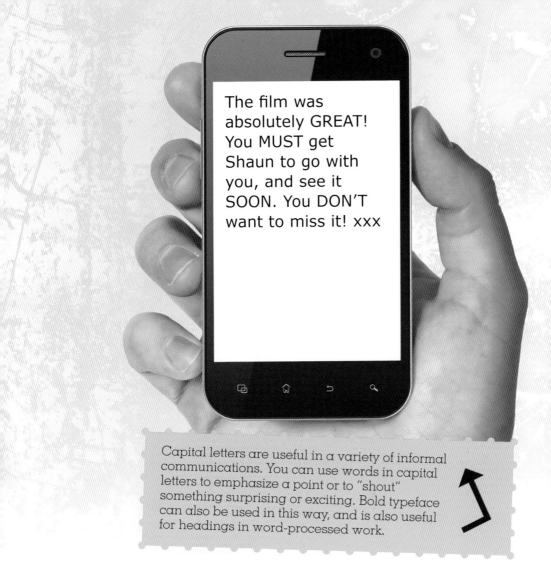

Capital letters are useful in a variety of informal communications. You can use words in capital letters to emphasize a point or to "shout" something surprising or exciting. Bold typeface can also be used in this way, and is also useful for headings in word-processed work.

Using the full stop in abbreviations

As well as ending sentences, full stops are also used in some abbreviations. These are shortened forms of words. Titles are often abbreviated, and some use full stops. The usual rule is that if the word being abbreviated still has its first and last letter, then it doesn't need a full stop. Examples are: Mr (Mister), Mrs (Missus), Dr (Doctor), Revd (Reverend), and St (Saint). Abbreviated titles that do need full stops include Prof. (Professor) and Rev. (Reverend).

Some abbreviations from Latin that are used in English always have full stops. These include e.g. (for example), etc. (and so forth), and i.e. (in other words). The full stop is also used to separate the hour from the minutes in time: 2.35 a.m.

Spelling in English is not easy. Unlike many languages, such as Italian and Spanish, words in English are often not spelled as they sound. The same letters can have many different pronunciations, and some of them can only be described as weird!

Can rules help?

There are many spelling rules in English that are helpful with certain word formations but, once again, it's not that straightforward. All English spelling rules have exceptions. With some rules, there seem to be more words that are exceptions than there are words that follow the rule. Some of the rules that work for many words are on the following pages.

Tricking your brain

There is nothing new about people finding English spelling difficult. Since this is the case, memory tricks and little sayings have been developed to help. These are known as mnemonics, and are explained on pages 34–36.

Memorizing is boring, but it works

There is sometimes no better way to learn spelling than by memorization. Carefully learning lists of spellings may seem boring, but it can give you a good framework of words you feel confident about. Try to focus on words you know you find hard.

EAT YOUR WORDS

Bad spelling can equal bad vocabulary!

Never let uncertainty about spelling keep you from using the best words you can. For example, if you want to describe how it feels to snowboard down an exciting slope, you don't want to say something boring like I went down the big mountain just because you can't spell more descriptive words. By learning spelling rules, using memory tricks, and consulting a good dictionary you could come up with I glided effortlessly down the precipitous slope.

There is help out there

Help with spelling is available from many sources. Dictionaries in print, online, and as apps are a good place to start. Lists of often misspelled words, like the ones on page 52, can also be useful. Don't forget to pay attention to the wiggly red lines under words in word-processed writing. These point out words the software thinks have been misspelled. You need to be careful how you select the correct replacement word. It's easy to click the first option and regret it later.

Never ignore it when your word processor points up a misspelled word, and be careful that you choose the right replacement. Remember, incorrectly used words that are correctly spelled might not be caught in a spellcheck – but they are still wrong!

Deer An,

Hit wars niece two sea ewe last weak . . .

Mnemonics: memory tricks to help you remember

The word mnemonic comes from the Greek word for memory. These memory tricks can be used to help you remember the correct spellings of words you find difficult. Here are some useful and interesting ones.

Looking for letters

One trick is to use the pronunciation of a word to help you remember how to spell it. In order for this method to work, you must pronounce all the letters in the word. For example, the word Arctic is often misspelled by the middle c being left out. Here is a mnemonic to help you remember it: The Arctic is cold. Purposely stressing the pronunciation of the c and then adding a related word beginning with c creates the mnemonic. Then, every time you need to spell Arctic, you bring this memory trick to mind.

Linking the c in the middle of Arctic to the word cold makes it more likely you will remember how to spell it … if you can remember that the Arctic is cold!

Here are a few more tricks to help you remember certain letters and meanings:

- The word visible is often misspelled. You can say, It is visible. I see it with my two eyes. Using this play on words helps you remember the "two eyes" (letter i) in the word.
- To remember whether desert or dessert is the correct spelling of the sweet pudding at the end of a meal, think of the fact that it is something extra, and dessert has an extra s.
- Principle and principal are two more words that are often confused. You can use bits from each to help you work out the correct spelling. You can say, The college principal is my **pal**. This helps you remember that principal ending in pal is the word that means chief, most important, or in charge. On the other hand, you can remember that A principle is a rule. The spelling of rule is the mnemonic to help you remember the meaning of the word when spelled with the -le ending.

Spelling it out

There are some memory tricks where every letter in the word is remembered by using the initial letters from words to make an interesting or amusing sentence. Here are two examples: Rhythm helps you to hear music – **rhythm**; Dash in a real rush. Hurry or else accident – **diarrhoea**.

Look at the frequently misspelled words on page 52. See if you can come up with your own mnemonic to help you remember the correct spellings for some of the words you are unsure of. You will be helping yourself on your way to spelling success.

Here is the "raven" trick to help you remember the right way to use two commonly misspelled and misused words:
RAVEN: remember, affect verb, effect noun.

So many exceptions: "i before e except after c"

One of the spelling rules that almost everyone learns is "i before e except after c". But what does this mean, and can you really use it to improve your spelling? The full rule is "i before e except after c when the ie is pronounced ee (as in seek)". There are many words that use this rule. Here are some examples: belief, field, niece, and grief. The after c exception words are also mostly where ei is pronounced like ee. These include receive, ceiling, and conceit. Getting this right can be very hard.

EAT YOUR WORDS
Help from crazy sentences!

These two sentences are called mnemonic devices. They might not make much sense, but they contain a lot of the exceptions to the "i before e" rule. See if you can make up one that contains more:

Neither leisured foreign neighbour seized the weird heights during the reign of their sovereign sheik, who held the reins of government.

The heir feigned that the neigh of either reindeer was due to the weight of eighty skeins of wool in the sleigh.

Sometimes, the sillier the mnemonic device, the easier it is to remember!

Four to remember

Is it -sede, -ceed, or -cede at the end of some words? In this case, learning four spelling exceptions will help you know the right way for all the rest. Only one word in the English language ends with -sede: supersede. Three words end with -ceed: exceed, proceed, and succeed. Memorize the spelling of these four words. All the others that sound like this end in -cede, such as concede, intercede, and precede.

SUPERSEDE

CONCEDE

INTERCEDE

PRECEDE

SUCCEED

EXCEED

PROCEED

It's lonely being the only English word to end in -sede. If I were an animal I'd be listed as very rare and endangered!

QUICK TIP

What does "cede" mean?

The **suffix** -cede is used to add the meaning "to go" or "to yield to". So, when used with pre- to form precede, it means "to go before". When added to re- to make recede, it means "to go back".

Three ways to help you get it right

When a rule has so many exceptions, there are three things you can do to help you spell correctly. Firstly, you can learn the spellings for those words you will use most often. Have a look at the most misspelled list on page 52. Top of the list of the "i before e" words that most people spell wrongly is receive, even though it follows the rule. The word their, which is an exception, is also often misspelled. So, learn those two and you already have a good start. Secondly, you can memorize some of the mnemonics that have been devised to help with exceptions to the rule (see page 36). Thirdly, when in doubt, check a good dictionary.

One of the trickiest areas of spelling in English is the fact that there are words that are pronounced the same, but spelled differently; words that are spelled the same, but mean completely different things; and words that are spelled the same way and pronounced differently – and have different meanings. These words are known as homonyms. Confused? It's not surprising! There are two types of same/different homonyms with their own special names:

- Homophones – These are words that sound the same, but are spelled differently and have different meanings.
- Homographs – These are words that are spelled the same way. They can be pronounced the same way or differently, but they do not have the same meaning.

Homophones: sound-alike words

Homophones often cause you to misspell, not because the word you are spelling doesn't exist, but because it isn't the word with the meaning you meant to use. For example, if you write a description of plants in a beautiful park or garden, then the word you mean to use is flower. However, if you are giving someone a recipe for a cake, the word you want to use is flour. They sound exactly the same, but are spelled differently and mean two very different things. There are hundreds of homophones in the English language, and it is difficult to learn them all. You can improve your spelling by making sure that you know the most commonly misused homophones.

This pair (meaning two) of pears (fruit) is an example of a homophone where the pronunciation of the words is the same, but the spelling and meaning are different.

Learn to, two, and too

To, two, and too are the most commonly used and misused homophones. This is what you need to remember about using them correctly:

Use to – This should be used to introduce a prepositional phrase, such as to the gig, in the sentence Chen and Annie went to the gig. It is also used in the infinitive form of a verb (the to form, such as to sing).

Use two – This should be used when you mean the number that comes after one, for example, in the sentence The two of them waited an hour for the bus after the gig finished.

Use too – This should be used when you mean "as well", or want to say that something is more than enough. Here are examples of both meanings: Jason has red hair, too. It comes down over his shoulders, which I think is too long.

Would you two like to cheerlead, too?

Just because words sound the same doesn't mean they have the same spelling, use, or definition!

Learn there, their, and they're

The other set of three homophones that causes the most trouble is there, their, and they're, which again sound the same, but have different meanings and spellings:

Use there – This should be used when you mean in a certain place, such as Jessie lives **there**. It is also used as an introductory adverb, for example, **There** is a time and place for loud music.

Use their – This determiner should be used when you are showing ownership or possession in the third person plural, such as **their** house, or **their** idea.

Use they're –This should only be used to show a contraction of the words they are, such as I think **they're** coming with us to the film.

EAT YOUR WORDS

All those vowels...

Some words sound right even when they are spelled wrong. That is because many vowels sound similar when you hear a word pronounced. For example, Ally made the mistake of thinking she could work out how to spell the word peasant. In a school exam she tried pesent, peasent, pesant, peasant, pesunt, and peasunt. Only one was right. A look in a dictionary would have made that clear!

same spelling

same pronunciation

bow
(to bend)

bow
(and arrow)

beau
(male beauty)

Bō
(city in
Sierra Leone)

As you can see, all but one of these words have the same pronunciation, only two are spelled the same way, and all of them have different meanings.

Homographs: look-alike words

Homographs are words that look exactly the same. In other words, their spelling is identical, but the meanings and sometimes the pronunciations are different. For example, the metal lead and the verb lead, meaning to guide or direct, look exactly the same, but are pronounced completely differently.

So, use of homographs will not lead to misspellings, but if you want to have a good vocabulary, you need to be aware of the fact that there are words like this. For example, here is a sentence using two words that are homographs and homophones. One is the name of a large type of mammal, and the other is a verb meaning the ability to put up with something: Could you bear being in a cage with a bear? In this case, there is also a third homophone word with a different spelling that means unclothed or uncovered: Could you bear being in a cage with a bear if you were bare?

How long can a bear bear being in a cage?

Homophones and homographs can make spelling tricky.

Spelling when you add to words

Affixes are the letters added to the beginning or end of main, or root, words to change them. The affixes used at the beginning, such as pre-, un- and re- , are called prefixes. Affixes used at the end, such as -s, -es, -ed, -ing, and -ly, are called suffixes.

Making nouns plural

In English, most nouns are made into plurals by adding s. These are called regular plurals. Unfortunately, there are many exceptions to this rule, which can lead to spelling mistakes.

Irregular plurals

One type of irregular plural is when the noun ends in an o. In this case, the rule is to add -es to make the word plural. Here are a few examples: potato to potatoes, tornado to tornadoes, and hero to heroes. This rule has almost more exceptions to the rule than words that follow it, including solo to solos, and piano to pianos. Some can even be made plural with either spelling, such as zero to zeros or zeroes, and halo to halos or haloes. So, unless you have learned and memorized an o plural, it is better to look a word up in the dictionary if you are in doubt.

When a noun ends in a y with a consonant in front of it, such as enemy, the y is changed to an i, and -es is added to make it plural: enemies. If the y has a vowel in front of it, such as monkey, then you only add an s like a regular plural: monkeys.

Making foreign words plural

Some words have come into English from other languages. Because of this, they do not make plurals in the normal way, but follow the rules from their original language. For example, to make axis plural, it is spelled axes; to make memorandum plural it is spelled memoranda; and to make cactus plural it is cacti! As you come across these words, you will need to learn how they make plurals, or just remember they are different and that you need to look them up.

Plurals in dictionaries

All good dictionaries will give the plural form of a word if it doesn't follow a recognized rule. For example, the entry for dog would not list a plural, as it is a regular noun that takes an s. However, there will be a mention of the plural form in the entry for banjo, which can be made plural either with an s or es. So, if there is no plural listed, you can presume that it isn't something strange.

Old words do it differently

Some of the oldest words in English, known as archaic or relic words, use unusual, old plural styles. Some, such as deer and sheep, are the same when singular or plural, so they are never deers or sheeps. Others use a different ending for their plural form, such as child to children or ox to oxen. Mouse becomes mice when plural, and goose becomes geese. Many of these ancient words are animal names. You can look up lists of relic words on the internet.

Some very old words in English, many originally from the Anglo-Saxon language, use unusual plural styles.

Apparently, we are so old that we don't need an s to make us plural.

The silent final e: to drop or not to drop

A big spelling pitfall is not knowing what to do when adding a suffix to the end of the main, or root word. In the case of words that end in a silent e, there are three spelling rules to learn that can help you:

- When a word ends with a silent e and you are adding an ending that begins with a vowel (-able, -ance, -ed, -er, -ible, -ing, or -ous), in most cases you drop the silent e. Here are some examples: come to coming, sense to sensible, grieve to grievous.
- When a word ends in a silent e, and you are adding an ending that begins with a consonant (-ness, -ment, -less, -ful, -ly) you usually keep the silent e. Here are some examples: move to movement, care to careful, love to lovely, tire to tireless. There are exceptions to this rule. Many of them occur when the letter before the silent e is another vowel, such as argue to argument and true to truly.
- When a word ends in -ce or -ge and you are adding -able or -ous, then keep the silent e. Here are a few examples: peace to peaceable, advantage to advantageous, and outrage to outrageous.

When a suffix is added to a root word ending with a silent e and the previous letter is a consonant, the e is often dropped, for example, fame to famous.

Some exceptions make sense

There are some silent e root words that keep the e when adding -ing. This is because dropping the e would be confusing as regards pronunciation, or could make one word look like another. For example, the word dying refers to someone or something becoming dead. The word dyeing refers to something having its colour changed. Keeping the silent e here makes it clear which word is being used.

Separated by a common language?

The written English of the United Kingdom and the USA differs in various respects. For example, British English prefers to use -our rather than -or in spelling (UK: colour, USA: color) and -re rather than -er (UK: theatre, USA: theater). Preferred British English style follows the silent e rule when adding -ment to judge and acknowledge and keeps the e (judgement and acknowledgement), whereas the US style makes exceptions of these and drops the e (judgment and acknowledgment).

No, Your Majesty, it's not misspelled – that's just American English.

British English and American English have many spelling differences. If you are using a spellcheck on your computer, tablet, or smartphone, make sure it is set for the correct form of English.

Deciding on double consonants

Another common spelling problem is knowing whether or not to double the consonant at the end of a word when adding an ending (suffix) or beginning (prefix). Fortunately, there are some useful rules that can help you:

- To add a suffix beginning with a vowel (-ing, -est) to a root word ending in a single consonant that is preceded by a single vowel, double the final consonant first. Here are some examples: swim to swimming, big to biggest, rob to robber.
- To add a suffix to a root word with more than one syllable that ends in a consonant, double the consonant only if the pronunciation accent is on the last syllable. Here are some examples: begin to beginning, control to controlling, admit to admitting. When the accent is not on the last syllable, then you do not double the final consonant: benefit to benefited, develop to developing.
- When you add the suffix -ly to root words that already end in l, then both are kept, such as normal to normally, forceful to forcefully, and usual to usually.
- The prefixes dis-, mis-, and un- each end with a single consonant. When you add them to root words that start with the same letter that the prefix ends in, both consonants are kept. Here are some examples: spell to misspell, natural to unnatural, satisfaction to dissatisfaction. If the end letter of the prefix and the first letter of the word it is being added to are **not** the same, there will be no double letters: agreeable to disagreeable, print to misprint, usual to unusual.

QUICK TIP

Where is the accent?

If you can't work out which syllable in a word is the accented, or stressed, syllable, say it out loud several times or get someone else to say it to you while you listen. If you still can't tell, check in a dictionary. The accented syllable is usually shown with a ' in the pronunciation guide for the word (see the dictionary sample on page 7).

When you add suffixes to the word swim, because it is one syllable and ends in a consonant preceded by a vowel, the final m is doubled as in swimming and swimmer.

QUICK TIP

One-syllable words

When you are adding -ly to one-syllable root words that end in y, sometimes both forms of spelling are acceptable: for example, dry with the suffix -ly is permissible as dryly and as drily. Check a dictionary to be sure.

Adding on to final y words

Words that end in y often cause problems for spellers when changes are made to them. Luckily, there are a few rules you can learn to help sort these problems out:

Forming plurals of words ending in y

When you want to make the plural of a word that ends in y, there are two rules to follow:

- When the y is preceded by a consonant – If this is the case, then the y should be changed to i and -es should be added: for example, poppy to poppies or diary to diaries.
- When the y is preceded by a vowel, leave the y and add s, for example valley to valleys or play to plays.

Rules for adding endings

There are three rules to learn about adding endings to words with a final y:

1. If the final y is preceded by a consonant, change the y to an i before adding endings that begin with a consonant. Here are some examples: beauty to beautiful, greedy to greedily, hungry to hungrily, penny to penniless.
2. Change the final y to an i before adding the endings -ed, -er, -es, and -est. Here are some examples: busy to busier, grumpy to grumpiest, occupy to occupied, satisfy to satisfies.
3. Keep the y before adding -ing, for example study to studying and hurry to hurrying.

EAT YOUR WORDS

More exceptions

As is the case with most spelling rules, there are exceptions when adding endings to words with a final y. Here are two where the final y is retained rather than changed to an i, even when the y follows a consonant: dry to dryness, sly to slyness. Here are a few examples where the y is changed to an i, even though it is preceded by a vowel: day to daily, pay to paid, slay to slain.

Root words that end in a y preceded by a consonant usually change the y to an i and add -es to become plural. Lilies, daisies, poppies, pansies, and peonies all become plurals by following this rule.

Adding k to final c words

Sometimes the spelling of a word is changed to preserve its pronunciation. This is the case when suffixes are added to verbs that end in c. If the suffixes -ed or -ing were added to a word like mimic to make it mimicing, it would look like other words that are pronounced with a soft c, such as dicing. In order to maintain it as a word that should be pronounced with a hard c, such as backing, a k is added before the suffix: mimicking. Here are some other examples where a k is added to words ending in c: picnic to picnicked and picnicking, and traffic to trafficked and trafficking.

QUICK TIP

Exceptions to the rules

There are also nouns that end in c, such as relic and picnic, but they do not have a k added when they are made plural: relics, picnics.

There are not many words in English that end in the letter c. Most are verbs, such as frolic. These lambs are frolicking in this field.

Practice makes perfect

Standard punctuation and spelling help to give our language a recognizable and understandable shape and appearance. It also makes it possible for others to learn and use our language. However, there are almost as many exceptions to the rules that govern English as there are rules themselves. The reasons for this are mainly historical, but writers, readers, speakers, and learners of English must embrace its diverse nature as it exists. The sheer quantity of English words, currently thought to number about 1 million, makes it hard for one person to know how to spell or punctuate all of them. But don't give up! By practising your writing skills, learning rules and memory tricks, and consulting good dictionaries, you can find your way with words.

English words can be very strange because of historical changes. For example, the old word for ship was skip. We might now say ship, but we still use the old word skipper, for the captain of a ship.

WORDS IN ACTION

Rules versus creativity

Spelling and punctuation rules don't exist to make writing boring. There is always a chance to develop original and inventive use of language – in the right place. Many authors and poets have bent the rules of grammar, punctuation, and spelling for creative reasons, including poet ee cummings (1894–1962), who felt that certain grammar rules, capital letters, and punctuation cramped his creativity. Here is part of one of his poems:

> when the oak begs permission of the birch
> to make an acorn – valleys accuse their
> mountains of having attitude – and march
> denounces april as a saboteur

From the poem *when serpents bargain for the right to squirm* by ee cummings, published in 1950 by Harcourt, Brace and World Inc.

accidentally
accommodation
acquaintance
all right
amateur
appearance
argument
believe
beneficial
benefited
buoyant
business
cemetery
committed
committee
competition
conscientious
conscious
criticism
deceive
definite
definitely
desert
desperate
dessert
develop
disappear
embarrassed
environment
exaggerate
exercise
familiar

February
focused
foreigner
fourth
government
grammar
grievance
heroes
humorous
imagination
interested
laboratory
library
lonely
loose
lose
losing
maintenance
marriage
mischievous
occasionally
occur
o'clock
omitted
opinion
parallel
parliament
personnel
pleasant
possess
precede
principal

principle
privilege
professor
quiet
quite
received
recommend
referred
remembrance
repellent
responsibility
restaurant
rhythm
schedule
seize
separate
siege
similar
society
stationery
succeed
successful
supersede
targeted
thousandth
transferred
villain
visible
Wednesday
weird
whether
yield

Glossary

abbreviation shortened version of a word or group of words using some of the letters in the original

accent stress placed on a syllable in a word

adjective word used to describe, or modify, a noun or pronoun

adverb word that describes, or modifies, a verb or another adverb

affix syllable or letter added to a word. When added at the beginning it is called a prefix. When added at the end it is called a suffix.

apostrophe punctuation mark used as a sign of an omitted letter or letters or to show possession

brackets pair of punctuation marks used to enclose words or figures

colon punctuation mark used before information introduced in the words that precede it

comma punctuation mark used in a sentence to create a short pause or separate off information

compound word word formed by combining two or more other words

consonant any of the non-vowel letters in the alphabet

contraction shortened form of a word or shortened combination of two or more words

determiner word that limits or modifies a noun and is the first word in a noun phrase

dialogue conversation between two or more people, or the spoken text of a script

ellipsis punctuation mark made of three dots used to represent omission or incompleteness

exclamation mark punctuation mark used to show surprise or a strong emphasis

fragment part of a sentence that does not contain both a subject and predicate and cannot stand on its own

full stop punctuation mark used to indicate the end of a sentence

grammar rules that deal with the structure of the words and sentences in a language

grammatical relating to grammar

homograph word that is spelled exactly like another word

homonym word that is either spelled like or sounds like another word

homophone word that sounds exactly like another word

hyphen punctuation mark used to join words or parts of words

infinitive verb in its simplest form, sometimes shown preceded by to

interjection word used to express an emotion or surprise, such as ouch! or help!

inverted commas see quotation marks

italic form of a typeface in which all the letters have a right-hand slant

main clause part of a sentence containing a subject and a predicate. A main clause can stand on its own as an independent sentence.

mnemonic method used to help remember something, such as a saying or acronym

modify use of a word or a group of words to describe or limit another word or group of words

noun word that names a person, place, thing, feeling, quality, or idea

omission marks see ellipsis

parentheses see round brackets

part of speech one of the types into which words are divided according to grammatical use

person term used to refer to the three categories of first person, second person, and third person

plural more than one

possessive showing possession or ownership

predicate part of a sentence made up of the main verb and words related to it

prefix letter or letters added to the beginning of a word

preposition word, such as above, from, and with, that shows the relationship between a noun or pronoun and other words in a sentence

pronoun one of the word types used in place of a noun

pronunciation how a word sounds when said out loud

punctuation special marks used to mark a sentence or words to make them clearer

question type of sentence that asks something which requires an answer

question mark punctuation mark used to show a sentence is asking something which requires an answer

quotation marks punctuation marks used to set off a direct quotation or spoken words, or to emphasize a word or phrase

root word form of a word with no prefixes or suffixes added. It is also known as a stem word.

round brackets curved pair of punctuation marks used to enclose words or figures

run-on term used to describe a sentence where two main clauses that could stand on their own are run together without proper punctuation

semicolon punctuation mark used primarily to divide two main clauses

sentence grammatical unit containing a subject and a predicate

singular no more than one

speech marks see quotation marks

spellchecker computer program which can be used to check the accuracy of a document's spelling

subject part of a sentence made up of the main noun and the words related to it

suffix letter or letters added to the end of a word

syntax structure of a sentence

verb word that expresses the action or state of being of a noun or pronoun

vowel letters a, e, i, o, u, and sometimes y. All the other letters are called consonants.

Find out more

Books

Accomodating Brocolli in the Cemetary or Why Can't Anybody Spell?, Vivian Cook (Profile Books, 2005)

Eats, Shoots and Leaves: The Zero Tolerance Approach to Punctuation, Lynne Truss (Profile Books, 2003)

i before e (except after c): Old-school Ways to Remember Stuff, Judy Parkinson (Michael O'Mara Books, 2007)

Key Stage 3 English: The Scary Bits, Richard Parsons (CGP Books, 2009)

Organizing and Using Information (Information Literacy Skills), Donald Aldcock & Beth Pulver (Heinemann Library, 2009)

Oxford School Dictionary and Thesaurus (Oxford University Press, 2012)

Write for Success (Life Skills), Jim Mack (Heinemann Library, 2009)

Websites

www.bbc.co.uk/schools/ks3bitesize/english/
This BBC website helps you revisit all the aspects of English you have studied at school.

www.bbc.co.uk/skillswise/topic/punctuation
Here you can explore in detail all the different punctuation marks and how to use them effectively.

Help yourself!

There are many ways in which you can help yourself improve your knowledge and skills in punctuation and spelling.

- There are workbooks available for you to use to deepen your understanding of punctuation and spelling.
- You can download printable worksheets from the internet that will help you practise punctuating sentences.
- There are many lists of spelling words for you to learn and test yourself on.
- Try to make your own list of spelling rules. Only you know the words that you always find hard to get right. Make your learning more interesting and easier to remember by creating crazy sentences or other mnemonic devices.

Index